# BUILDING BLOCKS
# FOR COMMUNICATION

## ACTIVITIES FOR PROMOTING LANGUAGE AND COMMUNICATION SKILLS IN CHILDREN WITH SPECIAL EDUCATIONAL NEEDS

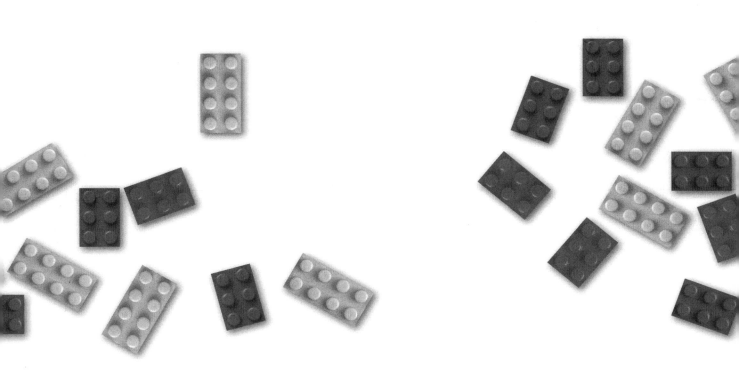

## Amy Eleftheriades

Speechmark

First published in 2015 by

**Speechmark Publishing Ltd**,

5 Thomas More Square, London E1W 1YW United Kingdom

**www.speechmark.net**

**002-5998** Printed in the United Kingdom by CMP (uk) Ltd

Design and artwork by Moo Creative (Luton)

British Library Cataloguing in Publication Data
A catalogue record for this book is available from the British Library

ISBN: 978 1 90930 137 5

# Contents

# Contents

# Acknowledgements

A huge thank you to all the children, young people, parents and practitioners who have played building blocks games with me over the years.

Also, a special thanks to staff at Stradbroke CEVC Primary School in Suffolk and the staff of Short Stay School for Norfolk, whose enthusiasm for Building Blocks sessions is inspiring!

Finally, thanks to Sally for being there and Teague for his ongoing support and, of course, the title.

**1**

# INTRODUCTION

# Introduction

Communication is so important. We use it in every aspect of our lives. It is not just about what we do or don't say; it is also about how we say it.

To be able to teach children how to communicate effectively, as practitioners, we need to start to think about it. How do we choose which words to use? How do we communicate in different contexts? How do we manage our communication to avoid misunderstandings? What do we do both consciously and automatically to improve our communication skills? Once we understand and are aware of these things, we can teach children how they can do the same.

There are a variety of resources available to practitioners to help guide them in the different aspects of language and communication. Before delivering sessions with children to help improve their language and communication skills, it is important to be clear what the nature of the difficulty is. Many tools and resources are available to help practitioners identify specific language and communication difficulties.

# Why use building blocks?

Lego™ and other building blocks are fun! They are an accessible tool that children (and adults) of all ages can engage with and which is often something that is familiar to them. Although the activities are structured for learning particular skills, the use of building blocks allows children to feel comfortable and relaxed while learning.

For a kinaesthetic learner, experiencing the lesson is extremely important. Building blocks offer children the opportunity to practise their communication skills while engaging in activities and, for this type of learner, it means they can make sense of their learning through 'doing'.

Building blocks make sense in a logical way. For children and young people who are logical thinkers, or for those who have autism or related conditions, concepts and language are often hard to understand. Using building blocks to help make the abstract more concrete gives meaning to language and communication and can often allow the logical thinker to feel more comfortable expressing themselves.

There are often children who struggle to sit quietly without fiddling. Many children with ADHD and other related conditions are 'on the go' and find it easier to focus when engaged in a practical activity. There are also many children who find that they feel more relaxed when they are engaged in practical activities. Building blocks are a great medium for this energy to be released productively.

Pushing bricks together and making models is great for improving fine motor skills in all children.

Using building blocks is creative and concrete. It allows children to see their success. This is especially important for those children who suffer from low self-esteem and struggle to see any positives in their work. For a child who doesn't like looking at their messy handwriting or the wrong answers in their book, working with building blocks offers the chance to create something that has no 'right' or 'wrong' and is unlimited in its variety of expression.

Children's level of engagement in these activities means they are more likely to remain focused on the task, even when it becomes challenging. The determination to complete a model or find the right piece often outweighs the uncomfortable feeling they're experiencing, so their ability to persevere and their resilience increases: 'Remember when you kept going with building that model, even when it was tricky – it shows you can persevere at a challenging task, and succeed!'

As practitioners we have an aim to the activity: the skills we are teaching through it. For the children, they are playing with building blocks with their friends and classmates.

# How to use this book

In this section you will find information about the different kinds of activities included, some ideas on how to run your sessions and reasons why building blocks can be educational as well as fun!

The activities are divided into four sections: Receptive and Expressive Language (Section 2), Social Language and Communication (Section 3), Language for Literacy (Section 4) and Language for Numeracy (Section 5). Inevitably, there will be activities that may cross over and can be used in a number of ways, so do explore.

As the activities have been designed to focus on different areas of language and communication, some may not seem right for the level that your children and young people are working at. Please look again! Most of the activities can be 'tweaked' to become more or less challenging by adding visual cues or putting restrictions on how they are played. Try presenting them in a slightly different manner, adding a time limit or increasing the independent working, and you will be able to run the game at the right level for your children.

The Appendix is an assortment of templates to use with some of the activities. They are designed as examples only and do not contain an exhaustive list of the vocabulary you may want to teach your children. You will also need a range of word, colour and number cards to use with the activities. Creating your own, personalised resources (time permitting!) will mean your children get the specific input and support they need. For example, reduce the number of words you have in a word bank, photocopy them on to coloured paper to make them easier to read and add your own variations of instructions, poems and playing cards.

You know your children best!

## Receptive and expressive language

Afasic explains receptive language as: 'the ability to understand or comprehend language heard or read' (Afasic, n.d.). It refers to the meaning, understanding and decoding of language. A child struggling with receptive language may find it difficult to understand what is being asked of them or misunderstand other people's spoken or written language.

Expressive language means 'being able to put thoughts into words and sentences, in a way that makes sense and is grammatically accurate' (Afasic, n.d.). Children may have speech problems that are preventing them from saying what they want, or they may be able to speak but struggle to put words into sentences in a grammatically correct way. There are also some children who are extremely good at saying words and who understand how to speak in a grammatically correct manner, but may need support to extend their vocabulary and become better at expressing themselves articulately.

The activities in this section have been designed to offer opportunities for children to practise listening, attending and responding to others and having the space and guidance to learn to express themselves well.

## Social language and communication

Many children are extremely good at speaking and have a good grasp of the language they use. These children may do well academically and show a good understanding of what is expected of them in particular situations, such as lessons in school or presenting a speech to an audience. They may, however, struggle to communicate well in a social context.

Social language and communication require a very particular kind of understanding. They require us to understand not only what is 'right' and 'wrong' in a factual or logical way, but also what is appropriate and inappropriate socially. Think about the last time you met someone you know. Did you give them a hug? Why, or why not? How did you know what you should do? When did you last laugh at a joke? Did everyone find it funny? Many children struggle to interpret social language and communication cues and this can cause many problems if they are not given the opportunity to learn about them explicitly. They will need time and a safe place to practise their social communication skills and learn appropriate ways to converse with others.

The activities in this section are designed to help teach children how to understand, explore and communicate feelings, thoughts and ideas in an appropriate way. They will also help children work together, taking turns in conversations and getting their point across politely and confidently.

## Language for literacy and numeracy

In order for children to understand what is being taught, they need to understand what is being said. Many children have gaps in their knowledge of key words which, if left unlearned, could cause problems throughout their education and later life.

A good understanding of the vocabulary used in basic literacy and numeracy will lay the foundations for a better understanding of concepts and skills needed to succeed both in and out of school.

Some children will need to learn this vocabulary explicitly and with more repetition than their peers. More practice and exposure to key terminology will aid them in their ongoing learning in the classroom and through life.

The activities in these sections offer a range of ideas on how to use building bricks to help teach vocabulary and extend descriptive language. It is not exhaustive and once you get going you will find many more ways to make their learning fun with the bricks!

## What do you see?

Many children with language and communication difficulties, whether diagnosed or not, can start to display a range of behaviours; some of which may be disruptive to others and some where you may find the child starts to withdraw from activities or situations.

The following pages are designed as an aid to considering where a language and communication problem may lie. They are not intended to be assessment tools to identify specific issues. To gain a better understanding of the nature of different speech, language and communication difficulties, visit the Afasic website: www. afasic.org.uk

Some things to consider before using activities to practise language and communication skills:

- Has the child been tested for hearing difficulties?

| Together they ran | sure they had got |
| through the streets | far enough away. |
| until they were | |

- Has the child been tested for sight difficulties?

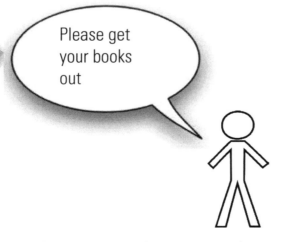

- Are they attending to the spoken word?

- Do they have knowledge of the words being used?

- Are they misunderstanding the meaning of the words?

- Can they remember a string of words?

- Do they struggle to say words correctly?

- Are they better at non-verbal tasks than verbal tasks? Do they have the information in their head but struggle to express themselves correctly?

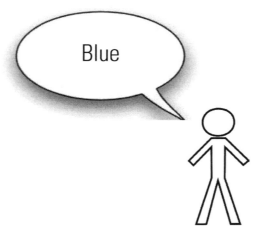

- Can they give answers correctly but only using single words?

- Do they use the correct words but struggle to put them in a grammatically correct sentence?

- Do they know how to speak well but are not confident or have extreme anxiety in speaking in front of others?

| Comment | Logically | Socially |
|---|---|---|
| 'He's really fat.' | ☺ | ☹ |
| 'I am better at spellings than everyone else.' | ☺ | ☹ |
| 'I think your drawing is really good.' | ☺ | ☺ |

- Do they get it 'right' logically but get it 'wrong' socially?

Once we know where the problem lies, as practitioners we can set appropriate targets and find activities, strategies and resources that will address the specific issues.

## Teaching communication

The children we work with may know that things seem to go wrong when they are talking with others, but they may not know why or what they can do to improve their experiences.

Below are two flowcharts that can be used while talking to the children about why it is important to learn to communicate well, and some tips on what they can do to help others understand them better.

**Communication check 1**

## Did I hear the words?

**YES
GREAT!**

**NO**

It is OK if I haven't heard. I can ask the person politely to repeat what they said – 'Please can you say that again, I didn't hear. Thank you.'

## Did I understand each of the words?

**YES
GREAT!**

**NO**

If there is a word I don't understand, it is OK to ask what it means – 'Can you tell me what ........ means please, I don't know that word.'

Did I understand what the person meant?

**YES**

**GREAT!**

**NO**

It is OK if I have understood most of the words but not what the person means. I can ask them to help me – 'Sorry, I don't understand what you mean, can you give me some more information please or explain in a different way?'

I can also check body language or other clues to see if I can understand what is being said. Are they pointing? Is their face giving me a 'secret' message about what they mean?

**Communication check 2**

Did the other person hear what I said??

**YES**
**GREAT!**

**NO**

It is OK if I repeat myself, speaking louder and taking time to say each word clearly.

I can try to get someone's attention by saying their name first.

Did they understand each of the words?

**YES**
**GREAT!**

**NO**

Not everyone will understand all of the words I use. I can check if they have understood by saying 'Did you understand what I meant by ...?'

Can I find another word that means the same thing to help them understand better? Can I describe what I mean? Eg a 'stud' is what I call the round circles on top of the block.

Did they seem to understand all of the information I gave them?

**YES**

**GREAT!**

**NO**

It is OK if someone doesn't understand what I say. I may have to find another way to help them.

Have I used words that could mean something else? Eg 'turn it round' could mean 'turn the whole model upside down' or 'turn it towards me'.

If they aren't doing what I expected, I can ask if they have understood or if they would like me to explain in a different way.

# Top tips for planning, delivering and monitoring activities

As practitioners, one of the most useful tools we have is the relationship we build with the children we work with. Everyone has their own style of delivering activities and it is important to feel comfortable and confident as the adult facilitating the session. How you want to structure your sessions will depend on your knowledge of the children; who they work best with, how long they can remain on task, what the signs are that they are starting to find something difficult and the ways they feel comfortable working.

The following are a few tips on things to consider to help your sessions run as smoothly as they can, whether you are delivering individual work or group activities. If you're interested in structuring your sessions further, you could take a look at the ebook *Interventions with Impact* (Eleftheriades, 2013).

## Planning

1   Start with the target – what does this child need to work on? Are the targets achievable for this child in the time I have to deliver the sessions? What do the children, parents and other practitioners think? Are the expectations high?

2   Think about activities – do they focus on my targets? Are they a good length for my sessions? Are they engaging?

3   Check with others – are the parents and other practitioners happy with the plan?

4   Think about the practicalities – do I have all the resources I need and the space to deliver the sessions? Where will they run, and how often?

## Delivery

1   Structure the sessions – think about ways to get the child in and settled ready for the session. Do I need a 'warm-up' game to start? Do they need some 'free play time' to unwind after the activities? Do they need a checklist to know what we will be doing? (See Appendix for a sample session checklist.)

2   Explain the rules – make sure there are clear rules about expectations and what the consequences are if there are any issues. Keep expectations high while allowing for the children to re-engage when appropriate. Do they need a visual reminder of the rules? (See Appendix for a sample session rules.)

3   Explain the expectations – do the children know what they need to do? Do the children know what skills or new vocabulary they are learning in this activity? Have I given them a chance to ask if they are unsure? Do they need a visual reminder? (See Appendix for sample secret challenges.)

4   Keep it fun!

5   Allow for emotions – do the children know what they can do if they are struggling to manage their feelings? Is there a separate chair to sit on for some 'time out' so they can calm down and re-engage when ready? Are there other, personalised strategies or resources that I can encourage them to use?

6   Allow for some free play at the end of each session – although the activities will feel like playing, they should also be challenging and the children will need to have the chance to play with the building blocks in their own way at the end of each session.

7   Clear up – do the children take responsibility for clearing up at the end of each session?

8   Language link – are there any new skills or vocabulary that the children can practise in other contexts such as the classroom or at home? Can I encourage them to transfer their learning in all areas of their lives?

## Monitor and review

1   Make notes – can I jot down things I see in the session, eg new words used, appropriate communication with others, etc? Do they link to the children's targets or are there other skills being learned?

2   Check the sessions – are they engaging? Do all the children take part? Who can I ask to observe and monitor my delivery? Are the sessions teaching the skills I planned for?

3   Pass on information – are there new strategies for helping the children that can be used in other contexts? Can I pass this information on to parents, other practitioners, etc?

4   Share progress – are the children improving their language and communication skills? Do their parents and other practitioners know this and do they see this in other contexts, eg at home or in the playground or classroom?

5    Review success – have the children achieved the targets set? Were the targets achievable and realistic? Are there other underlying speech and language

issues that need to be assessed by other professionals? Do the children know what they have achieved? Can they give specific examples?

6  Celebrate success – can I have a celebration session and invite parents and others to join? How can we display or present what the children have achieved?

7  Next steps – do the children still require these sessions? What will be their new targets? What do the children, parents and other professionals think?

# References

Afasic (n.d.) 'Receptive and expressive language', online, www.afasic.org.uk/recognising-a-problem/speech-language-and-communication/receptive-and-expressive-language/ (accessed March 2015).

Eleftheriades A (2013) *Interventions with Impact: Plan, Run and Evaluate Effective Pupil Interventions*, Optimus Education, online, www.optimus-education.com/shop/interventions-impact-plan-run-and-evaluate-effective-pupil-interventions (accessed March 2015).

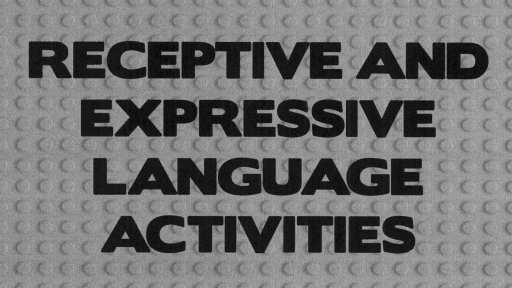

# 2

# RECEPTIVE AND EXPRESSIVE LANGUAGE ACTIVITIES

# Simple sorting

## Aim

- To follow instructions
- To work with others

## Assessment opportunities

This activity will help identify specific gaps in understanding, such as knowledge of colours, shapes, relative sizes, etc.

## What you need

- Pile of building bricks and pieces
- Descriptive word cards if needed (see Appendix for example)

## ACTIVITY

Put the building bricks and pieces into the middle of the table.

Explain to the children that they need to sort them by colour. Give them the opportunity to discuss the variety of colours together. There may be pieces that have more than one colour. Allow the children to problem solve around these bricks, prompting discussion as a group. If they are struggling, you may want to encourage them to ask for your help and offer a number of ideas which they can choose from. For example, 'Do you think that this piece can be placed with the reds, because although it has some green on it, it is mostly red? Or shall we create a pile for the bricks with more than one colour on?'

Repeat the activity, asking the children to sort the pieces by shape. Once again, allow the discussion about what shapes they have.

Finally, ask the children to sort in any way they want. Facilitate discussions about different options and ways they could sort, and help them manage to compromise so that they can agree on a particular way.

## Variations

Use other ways to sort to make it more challenging. See also the next activity, 'Complex sorting'.

# Complex sorting

## Aim
- To follow instructions
- To discuss ideas within a group

## Assessment opportunities
This activity will help identify any difficulties understanding abstract concepts and making connections.

## What you need
- Pile of building bricks, wheels, people, windows, vehicles, etc.

## ACTIVITY
Ask the children to sort the building bricks by function of the pieces.

Give them the opportunity to discuss the bricks and other pieces and decide on categories. They may need some help to do this in an appropriate way. Model ways to compromise and manage feelings of disappointment if their categories are not chosen.

Categories may include (but not be restricted to): wheels, vehicles, people, building bricks, etc. There may be pieces that could fit into more than one category. Encourage the children to problem solve around these pieces, prompting discussion as a group. If they are struggling, you may want to encourage them to ask for your help and offer a number of ideas they can choose from.

## Variations
Extend thinking and understanding of abstract concepts further. For instance, you can ask the children to sort in other ways, such as 'usefulness at a party or on a desert island' (extremely useful, useful, not very useful, completely useless).

# Match the piece

## Aim

- To use well-formed sentences with descriptive language

## Assessment opportunities

This activity will help identify children who find it difficult to speak in whole sentences.

## What you need

- Two piles of bricks and pieces with the same amount and style of bricks in each pile

- Vocab cards and word banks (if required) (see Appendix for examples)

- Small bag

## ACTIVITY

Put one of the piles of bricks into the bag. Place the other across the middle of the table.

Explain that they are going to take it in turns to pull a piece from the bag and they need to see if they can find the matching piece on the table. Model doing this first, using whole sentences to describe the piece and giving the children time to look for the matching one on the table. When you have found the correct piece, repeat the process of describing its features to check you are right.

The children should have a go at the same activity, describing the piece and finding its matching pair.

Encourage teamwork, with the children asking others for help with descriptive words if needed.

## Variations

When the children are confident, start to add in more imaginative descriptive terms such as 'It looks like a little blue box.'

# Building bricks bingo

## Aim

• To listen carefully and understand descriptive terms

## Assessment opportunities

This activity will help identify the children who find it difficult to process verbal information.

## What you need

• Camera

• Bingo grids (see Appendix)

• Scissors

• Glue

• Variety of building bricks, pieces, vehicles and figures

• Counters

## Before starting the activity

Make the bingo cards (can be prepared beforehand if necessary):

Explain to the children they are going to make a building bricks bingo game. They should pick a few pieces each.

In pairs, they should help each other take photos of their pieces. Encourage the children to discuss the pieces as they take photos of them – what colours and shapes they are and how many studs (dots) they have on them.

Print out the photos – more than one of each photo will need to be printed out.

Get the children to cut out and stick the photos on to the bingo grids.

## ACTIVITY

Each player should have a bingo card. Ask the children to say the names of the colours and shapes they see. Use a word bank if needed.

Pick out a piece from the bag and describe it to the group. The children should listen and look at their cards to see if they have the same piece on their card. If they do, they can cover that picture up with a counter.

When someone has successfully covered a line on their card, they should shout 'BINGO' and receive a reward. The game should continue until someone successfully covers all of their pictures of pieces and shouts 'FULL HOUSE' to receive a reward.

The children can play the game again, taking it in turns to be the 'bingo caller'.

## Variations

To make the game more difficult, the facilitator can keep the pieces hidden in the bag while describing them, so the children are relying solely on their listening skills to identify the correct pieces.

# Listen and build

## Aim
- To listen carefully
- To follow instructions

## Assessment opportunities

This activity offers opportunities to assess the knowledge of colour and shape words.

It will also highlight if any children struggle with working memory, finding it difficult to follow more than one instruction at a time.

## What you need
- Pile of building bricks which should include all those specified on the listen and build cards
- Listen and build cards (see Appendix for examples)

## ACTIVITY

The pile of bricks should be in the middle.

Read out the instructions on the first card and each child should collect the pieces needed and build a model. Put a time limit on the building of the model to keep the pace of the activity going.

Once built, read out the 'Listen and build' card again and allow the children to check their model to make sure they have included all the pieces needed. If they haven't, give them the opportunity to correct their model.

Repeat the activity using another card. The difficulty level can be increased by picking cards with more information and a greater variety of pieces.

When they are confident, the children can work in pairs to give each other instructions.

## Variations

If needed, make it easier by making the cards visible to the group. This will mean they can check the pieces needed and not have to rely on working memory.

# Describe the card

## Aim

- To listen carefully

- To follow instructions

## Assessment opportunities

This activity offers opportunities to assess the ability to use descriptive words appropriately and in whole sentences.

## What you need

- About 20 building bricks and pieces

- Camera

- Laminator

- Word banks and vocab cards (see Appendix for example)

## Before starting the activity

Make the cards (can be prepared beforehand if required):

Explain to the children that they are going to make some playing cards for their game. They should take photos of each brick, helping each other to use the camera. Encourage the children to describe the bricks, using colour and shape words and other descriptive terms.

Print the photos out and laminate them or stick them on card.

## ACTIVITY

Each child has some of the bricks and pieces that have been used to make the cards.

The cards should be placed in the middle in a pile facing downwards. Model the process, picking up a card from the pile and describing the piece. Explain that you will be listening out for whole sentences being used to describe the piece. For example, 'I am looking for a red brick with six studs on. It has three rows of two studs and it is a cuboid.'

If needed, any of the vocab cards or word banks can be used to help remind children of the key words.

The children look at their pieces to see if they have the one being described. If they think they do, they should hold it up and if it matches the picture on the card, they pass it to the child who described the piece.

Encourage polite conversation skills at this point, prompting 'please' and 'thank you', and verbal as well as non-verbal communication. For example, 'Is this the piece you are looking for?'

Once all the cards have been used, the children can make a model using a larger pile of bricks.

## Variations

Add more challenging pieces that require new vocabulary. Children can work in pairs to describe the pieces, which may help to build confidence.

# What could it be?

## Aim

- To use imagination and creative description in sentences

## Assessment opportunities

This activity will help identify the children who struggle to use imaginative and descriptive language in sentences.

## What you need

- Pile of building bricks and pieces

## ACTIVITY

Put the pile of bricks and pieces in the middle.

Pick up a few bricks and put them together. Model to the children how we can be creative and have fun 'guessing' at what our little model could be. Use plenty of imagination and creative descriptive language. For example, 'This bright green piece looks like it could be the comfy armchair of a pixie prince.'

The children should have a go at the same activity, putting a few pieces together and describing their model in any way they like. Encourage the children to be very imaginative – there should be no limit on the creativity with this activity.

Get the children to repeat the activity and ask someone else to guess what their model could be.

## Variations

Use a vocab card with descriptive words on if the children need support initially.

# Buzz-in (simple)

## Aim

- To attend and listen to information

- To be able to give clear descriptions to others

## Assessment opportunities

This activity will help identify children who struggle to process verbal information. You may find some children will engage with the game but don't seem quick enough to respond to the information. They may be having difficulty processing the information at the speed of their peers. You can adapt the game to allow for this if needed.

## What you need

- Pile of building bricks

## ACTIVITY

Ask the children to decide on their 'buzz' sound. This can be any noise or sound, or you may decide to give them buzzers. If a child is uncomfortable with making a noise, they can tap the table with their hand to indicate they know the answer.

Ask the children to tell you the colours they can see in the pile. 'Collect' colour words, monitoring whether all the children are using the words correctly. Ask them to tell you the different shapes they see. Use word banks or vocab cards if needed. Ask the children how many studs (dots) they can see on top of different pieces. Check the accuracy and understanding of number.

Tell the children you will describe a piece from the pile. They should look and listen carefully. If they think they know which piece you are describing, they should 'buzz'. The child who guesses correctly gets the next go and the person describing the piece gets to keep the piece they successfully described.

Continue the game, encouraging innovative descriptive terms and modelling the use of new words if needed.

NB If a child is struggling to 'buzz-in' in time and is at risk of disengaging, you may want to take turns around the circle instead, to ensure everyone has a go.

## Variations

Silent buzz: use word cards instead of verbal description. The children can have a set of descriptive cards each and find and show the words to describe the piece. Make sure they have some blank cards so they can add their own descriptions.

# Buzz-in (complex)

## Aim

- To listen to and express descriptive words

- To work in a group – managing feelings

## Assessment opportunities

This activity will help identify children who have limited vocabulary and may be struggling to understand some conversations and instructions because they don't understand words.

## What you need

- A pile of building bricks

## ACTIVITY

As with the simple buzz-in game, ask the children to decide on their 'buzz' sound. Provide a buzzer if needed.

Model describing a piece from the pile. Tell the children that you are not allowed to use colour words, so you're going to have to work hard to think of some more interesting words to make sure they can understand you. An example might be: 'This piece is long and thin and the colour of the frog in the pond at the end of the garden.'

Ask the children to discuss some ideas of other descriptions they can use that don't include colour words. Encourage innovative ways to describe pieces.

Start the game by describing a piece. The child who guesses correctly gets the next go and the person *describing* the piece gets to keep the piece they successfully described.

Continue the game, encouraging the children to not take themselves too seriously and allowing time to discuss the terms used. Correct any misuse of words.

## Variations

Shape/number buzz-in: play the game with the children substituting shape or number words for new words or interesting terms.

# Speed swap

### Aim
- To listen carefully to instructions

### Assessment opportunities
This activity may help identify children who struggle to process information quickly. They will struggle to find the correct pieces in time to swap them and may become frustrated or disengage from the game. This game can be adapted to help these children practise at their level.

### What you need
- A pile of building bricks, vehicles, people and pieces
- Small piles of the same bricks/pieces for each player

### ACTIVITY
Give the children a small pile of bricks each. Initially make sure each player has the same pieces in their pile. Put a larger pile of bricks and pieces in the middle.

Call out a piece that is in the children's piles by describing it. Colour words, shapes and other descriptive terms can be used.

The players have to listen carefully and look at the pieces in their pile. If they think they know which piece is being called out, they can quickly swap it with a piece in the middle pile that they would like. Only the first player to spot the piece gets to swap.

This should continue until the facilitator is happy that all players have managed to listen carefully and swap pieces.

The children can have some time at the end of the game to build a model with their pieces and those from the main pile.

### Variations
If a player struggles to process the information about the description of the piece quickly enough, the game can be slowed down by the players taking it in turns to 'speed swap' with the pile in the middle and take the competitive element out of the game.

# Persuade me with pieces 1

## Aim

- To use persuasive language in expressing ideas

## Assessment opportunities

This activity will help identify the children who are not confident in expressing themselves verbally.

## What you need

- Pile of bricks and other pieces

- Paper and pens

## ACTIVITY

Talk about how we can use language and the way we talk to people to persuade others that we have important views and opinions.

Discuss the use of confident body language, such as use of eye contact, shoulders back, head up, projecting your voice, etc.

Discuss people who are good at this, eg world leaders, successful business people and others they may know personally.

Explain that they will be presented with a dilemma and they will have to construct a solution which they will then present to the rest of the group. The dilemma is:

*Someone is stuck on an island surrounded by shark-infested waters and needs help to construct a suitable piece of equipment to help them get off the island (NB this does not have to be a boat). They have some water but are quickly running out and they are also at risk of getting burnt by the sun. Design a piece of equipment to help.*

The children can use any pieces they need to construct a prototype of their design, paying careful attention to the necessary features.

Show the group how they can write the key facts of their model on paper to use as a prompt for when they deliver their presentation.

Ask each child to present their model, highlighting the main features of their design. Get the children to think about using confident body language and projecting their voice while discussing their model.

Ask the group to give positive feedback p    oints to each speaker for both their designs and the delivery of their presentations.

## Variations

For children who struggle to present to others, even in a small group, they could record their presentation alone in another room and play it to the group afterwards.

# Persuade me with pieces 2

## Aim

- To be persuasive in expressing ideas with a focus on voice tone, intonation, volume and use of silence to add impact

## Assessment opportunities

This activity will help identify the children who are not confident in expressing themselves verbally.

## What you need

- Pile of bricks and other pieces

- Paper and pens

## ACTIVITY

Discuss how using confident body language, such as eye contact, shoulders back, head up, projecting our voice, etc can affect how we come across when explaining our ideas. Discuss how changing tone of voice, pausing at specific points in a speech and raising and lowering the volume of the voice can add impact to speeches. You can model this.

Explain to the children that they will be presented with a dilemma and they will have to construct a solution which they will then present to the rest of the group. The focus will be on how they use their voice to change the dynamics of their presentation. The dilemma is:

*A group of explorers have arrived at the North Pole and need a suitable design for the buildings they want to construct. The buildings should not only protect them from the freezing cold temperatures but should be able to be transported quickly and easily if needed. It also needs to have features to keep the explorers safe from visits from inquisitive wildlife.*

The children can use any pieces they need to construct a prototype of their design. They can practise their speeches in pairs, giving each other constructive criticism and pointers on how to change their delivery to be more persuasive.

Ask each child to present their model, highlighting the main features of their design with attention to how they use their voice and pauses to add impact.

Ask the group to give positive feedback points to each speaker for the delivery of their presentations.

## Variations

As with the 'Persuade me with pieces 1' activity, children who struggle to present to others, even in a small group, can record their presentation alone in another room and play it to the group afterwards.

# 3

# SOCIAL LANGUAGE AND COMMUNICATION ACTIVITIES

# This is me

### Aim
- To appropriately communicate thoughts and ideas

### Assessment opportunities
This activity will help identify children who struggle with self-awareness.

### What you need
- A pile of building bricks, vehicles, figures and pieces

### ACTIVITY
Build a simple model which represents yourself. This could include figures which represent family members, a model of your favourite place and/or particular pieces that represent things you are good at and things you like and don't like.

Talk about the different aspects of the model and how they link to things about yourself.

Ask the children to use any of the pieces from the pile to construct a model that represents themselves. If they struggle to identify things, you could ask questions to help promote thinking, such as 'What might your friend say you like to do?' or 'Which lessons do you like?'

When the models have been built, encourage the children to share their model with the person sitting next to them, describing how it represents them and who they are. Encourage some children to share their model with the group, making it clear that it is not compulsory and they should only share if they are comfortable doing so.

### Variations
Some children may struggle to share their model in a group. This activity can be done as individual or pair work until the child is comfortable sharing in a group.

# Colourful feelings

## Aim

- To understand and communicate feelings

- Listening to others

## Assessment opportunities

This activity will help identify children who have a limited vocabulary for feelings and emotional language. The activity can be adapted to help these children learn about the words before learning how to communicate them appropriately.

## What you need

- A pile of building bricks which include a large amount of each colour

- Small figures

- Large pieces of paper and coloured pens

## ACTIVITY

Talk with the children about feelings. Ask them to name feelings that they know, eg happy, tired, angry, excited, etc. Write them on a large piece of paper, using a different colour for each feeling. Then let the children do the same on their own paper, deciding which colour will go with each feeling for them. It is OK if these colours are different for each child.

If the group are finding it difficult to name feelings, add some for them, giving examples of when someone may experience this feeling. For example, 'Someone may get disappointed if they don't get picked to answer a question in class', or 'Someone may get worried if they don't understand what the task is'.

Let each child have a pile of bricks of each colour, putting them on their paper on top of the corresponding feeling. Let them choose a small figure each.

Explain that the children should think about a time they felt a particular feeling. Get the children to build a model showing an event or memory of this time, using the corresponding colour bricks.

Once completed, ask each child to describe their model, using their figure to represent themselves, 'walking' it through their scenario.

Repeat the activity with a different feeling.

## Variations

Some children will still struggle to describe their feelings in a group. If this is the case, this activity can be done one-to-one first and later repeated within a group in order for these children to get used to the process.

# Hopes and wishes

### Aim
• To appropriately communicate thoughts and ideas

### Assessment opportunities
This activity will help identify children who find it difficult to express their ideas.

### What you need
• A pile of building bricks, vehicles, people and pieces

### ACTIVITY
Build a simple model which represents something you hope for the future. Describe to the group what the model means to you and the reasons for your choice. An example might be a model that represents working hard to organise yourself better at weekends, so the 'boring' jobs get done first.

Ask the children to think about what they would like to improve on and build it with the pieces. Some children may need some help thinking about this and questions can be used to promote thinking, such as:

• Is there anything you can think of that you would like to achieve in the future?

• Think of someone you admire. What is it about them that you admire? Is this a quality or skill you would like?

• If you had a magic wand, is there anything you would like to change?

When the models have been built, ask the children to describe what they have built. Give the opportunity for discussion and ideas on how each person can move towards their goal with small steps.

### Variations
Some children will struggle to describe their goals, especially if they have low self-esteem and are concerned that they don't have the ability to achieve them. If this is the case, they should focus on the 'This is me' activity initially and then they should have the option of building a 'Hopes and wishes' model without the pressure of sharing it with others straight away.

# A week in bricks (self-assessment)

## Aims

- To be able to verbalise feelings about tasks and progress

## Assessment opportunities

This activity will help identify children who struggle to use traditional methods of self-assessment and need kinaesthetic methods to help them verbalise their thoughts.

## What you need

- A pile of building bricks, pieces, vehicles and figures

## ACTIVITY

Talk to the children about their recent experiences at home or school. Remind them of some of the lessons they have been in, projects they have completed or tasks they have finished.

With the building bricks in the middle of the table, ask the children to build:

1   Their favourite task this week

2   Their least favourite task this week

3   Something they got better at this week

4   Something they struggled with and want to get better at

After each model, ask the children to explain what they have built and encourage further description by asking questions about different parts of the model. Encourage other children to ask questions.

If needed, adjust the questioning to assess tasks for that day.

## Variations

If there is a good relationship between the children, ask them to build models of what they felt others in the group have done well (peer assessment).

# My house, my life

## Aim

- To be able to verbalise feelings about their life. Be aware that the children may open up about sensitive things and if this happens, ensure you follow the safeguarding policies of your organisation.

## Assessment opportunities

This activity will help identify children who struggle to verbalise how they feel about different aspects of their life.

## What you need

- A pile of building bricks, pieces, vehicles and figures

## ACTIVITY

Make sure that the children are aware that during this activity there is no pressure for them to share anything they don't want to – it may be difficult for the children to talk about difficult things. If this is the case, do this activity one-to-one rather than in a group situation. If they want to, the child or young person can just build the house and decide to talk about it another time, when they are ready.

Talk to the children about how we have 'ups' and 'downs' in life; things that are going well and make our lives good, and other things that might make us sad or worried.

The facilitator should model building a house and explain that this represents their life at the moment. Ask the children to build their own using any pieces they want.

Ask the children to add things to their house that make their life good. Get them to think about the people who are important in their lives and put figures representing them in or near their house. They can add things they like to do.

Ask the children to add things to their house that aren't as good, such as people or things that they worry about. If they are comfortable, the children can share their worries.

Ask the children to add things they would like to happen in their lives – hopes for the future.

Keep the houses safe and take photos of them for the children to put in a book.

Allow for some free play so the children can feel OK before leaving the session. Monitor their mood and communicate with colleagues if needed.

## Variations

This activity can be done in stages over a few weeks if needed, to allow for the children to share their feelings gradually over time.

# Steps to success

### Aim

- To think about small steps towards goals

### Assessment opportunities

This activity will help identify children who struggle to think about how to move towards targets.

### What you need

- A pile of building bricks, figures
- Paper and pens
- Blu-Tack

### ACTIVITY

Tell the children they are going to think about steps to success – with any goal they might have.

Build a model representing 'steps' using the building blocks. The steps may be different sizes and colours but always heading towards the goal at the top. Give an example of a goal, such as being able to work better in a group, or getting more work done in class.

Write this goal on a piece of paper and attach it to the top of the steps.

Explain that to reach this goal there will be things we can practise and try out. For example, working better in a group might mean small steps such as 'managing to sit next to others', 'waiting until someone else has finished speaking before I speak', 'calmly giving my opinion', 'helping someone else', etc. As we try these new skills we move closer to our goal – this can be represented with a small figure 'climbing' the steps.

Encourage the children to think about themselves; what they have already achieved and things they would like to get better at. For younger children, they might think about how they work in class or how they play outside with others. Older students may start thinking about what they want to do when they leave school or whether they'd like to have more friends.

Get the children to build their steps and put their goal at the top. They should think about what they already do that are steps towards their goal and acknowledge that they are on their way there already.

Discuss what other steps they could take.

This activity can be revisited at different points and the children can see how they continue to make small steps.

## Variations

If a child is struggling to consistently achieve the small steps, the model can be adjusted to show 'ups and downs' in reaching goals. The message should be that with perseverance and resilience, they can get there but it may take time and patience.

# The negotiator

## Aim

- To work with others, learning to compromise and express thoughts appropriately

## Assessment opportunities

This activity will help identify children who struggle to communicate appropriately while experiencing strong feelings. It will also help identify those who struggle to share and compromise with others in a social situation.

## What you need

- A pile of building bricks, vehicles, people and pieces

- The negotiator script cards (see Appendix for example)

## ACTIVITY

Give the children a pile of bricks each. Make sure each pile includes a number of interesting pieces and a mix of bricks.

Explain to the children that they will be building anything they want. If they see a piece they would like in someone else's pile, they will be able to negotiate to swap some pieces.

Explain what negotiation is. Go through the sentences on the negotiator script cards. Explain to the children that you will be listening out for these kinds of sentences being used. Be clear that the children are allowed to say no if they don't want to give up particular pieces. They are practising appropriate assertive communication: they do not have to hand over all their favourite pieces, but they have to be polite if saying no to someone's request.

Let the children play and have a go at negotiating. Give them time to practise their skills and help facilitate or prompt discussion as necessary.

Ask the children how it felt to negotiate and which sentences worked best for them.

## Variations

Get the children to create new negotiator cards as they learn new ways to negotiate.

Speechmark

# Pass the model

## Aim

- To learn to work well in a group

## Assessment opportunities

This activity will help identify children who struggle to manage other people's views and may be rigid in their thinking. The activity can be adapted to help these children learn how to manage different opinions and following someone else's ideas.

## What you need

- A pile of building bricks for each person

## ACTIVITY

Explain that the group will be building a model together. They will need to add two bricks to the model on their turn and then pass the model on to the next person. Explain that it is OK if others put pieces on that they wouldn't choose for the model. This is part of learning to work well as a team –compromising their own ideas so that it can be fair for everyone in the group.

Start to pass the model round and encourage the children to make a positive comment about others' choices when appropriate.

Ask the children to reflect on what it feels like when others were making choices that may have been different from theirs. Were they able to compliment someone else even if they didn't agree with their choice? Could they manage their feelings about it?

## Variations

You can restrict the types of bricks to be used in each go, for example only cubes or orange pieces. This may be harder for the children to manage if they had planned to use particular pieces, which will help them manage feelings of frustration and disappointment.

# More than one way

## Aim
- To be able to communicate ideas in a group and manage differences of opinion

## Assessment opportunities
This activity will help identify children who struggle to accept that others may have different opinions.

## What you need
- A pile of building bricks, vehicles, pieces

## ACTIVITY
Give each child a pile of bricks and pieces. Explain to the children you are going to give them some instructions on what to build and a time limit for when it should be completed by. They should build by themselves.

Give the first instruction – to build a tower in five minutes.

At the end of five minutes, ask the children to show the group their towers. Discuss how each of the towers is different. Ask the children to compare features, being clear that all have correctly followed the instructions. Explain that often there is not a clear 'right' or 'wrong' in life. Sometimes we perceive things differently and sometimes we have different opinions from others. Each person is allowed to have their opinion, and we have to try to respect it, even if we don't agree with it.

Ask the children to follow the next instruction – to build a vehicle. Again, compare the results and encourage the children to say a positive thing about each other's models.

Ask the children to come up with the next instruction. When the models have been built, ask them if all the models were built in the way they would have done it – does it matter? Can they give examples of where they have noticed they do things in a different way from their peers? How do they feel about it? Is there always a 'right' and 'wrong' way to do things?

## Variations
Give the children the chance to work in pairs, creating models from the same instruction.

# Create together

## Aim

• Managing compromise and appropriate social language in pair work

## Assessment opportunities

This activity will help identify children who are rigid in their thinking and struggle to let others have an input in group work.

## What you need

• A pile of building bricks

• 'Team speak' cards (see Appendix for example)

## ACTIVITY

Explain that the children will be building models in pairs. Discuss how it may feel to have someone else building with you. Talk about positive things that can come from working with others, such as extending ideas, learning to compromise, etc. Talk about how important it is to be able to get along with others, even when we don't agree with everything they say or do.

Talk through the 'Team speak' cards. Discuss how we can disagree about decisions other people make without appearing rude or inappropriate. Discuss how tone of voice and the 'way' things are said will affect how someone feels. Model using some sentences from the cards.

Children to build models together, practising the sentences on the cards. Note and praise children when they use the sentences appropriately.

After the activity, ask the children to explain how it felt and which sentences worked better for them.

## Variations

Run the activity again with three or four children in the group.

# Comic book collaboration

## Aim
- To work well in a group; contributing in a given role and compromising with ideas

## Assessment opportunities
This activity will help identify the children who struggle to manage working appropriately with others.

## What you need
- Building bricks, pieces, vehicles and figures
- Junk modelling/craft items
- Paper and pens
- 'Team speak' cards (see Appendix)
- Camera

## ACTIVITY
The children are going to create their own comic book, as a team. Discuss how it is often the case that if we work well together, we can achieve more than we would on our own. This is not always easy, but we can practise to get better at it.

Explain that there are different roles in creating a comic book. For this activity they will need:

- Story writers – this person or people will make decisions on the story. They will need to decide what will happen to the characters, draw the events out on a storyboard and communicate with the set designer on what the set may look like.

- Set designers – this person or people will listen to the story ideas from the writer and design and construct the set for the characters to 'act' in.

In pairs, they should decide who will take each role. The children should decide on where their comic book story is set and which characters they will have in it. If they have completed the 'Story building' activities (*see* pp64-70), they may want to use sets they have already built.

The children should complete their tasks with a focus on talking to each other to share information and their thoughts appropriately. The set designer should build the sets using the building bricks and junk modelling equipment, talking with the writer to help inform what the sets look like. The writer should draw out the story on the storyboard, talking with the set designer about their ideas.

Explain to the children they may want to use some of the sentences on the 'Team speak' cards. Tell them you will be listening to hear how they use them.

When the children have completed their tasks, they should use the figures to act out their story, taking photos of key points to use to create their comic book.

Print the photos and get the children to stick them in the correct order, writing captions underneath each photo to tell the story.

Ask the children to reflect on the process. Was it easy working together? What things worked well? What will they try to change next time?

## Variations
Other roles can be given if the children are working in small groups.

# Create a game

## Aim

- To work well in a group; designing and facilitating a game appropriately

## Assessment opportunities

This activity will help identify the children who struggle to manage to communicate appropriately within a group.

## What you need

- Building bricks, pieces, vehicles and figures
- Paper and pens

## ACTIVITY

Explain to the children that they will be designing their own building bricks game.

Tell them the game should:

- have a clear set of rules
- include everyone in the group.

The children should have a pile of building bricks each and create a game they will describe to the rest of the group. If a child struggles to create their own, they can work in pairs or receive help to create one.

The children should write out the rules of their game.

The children should take it in turns to describe their game to the group and have a go at playing it. The focus should be on the children being appropriately assertive and confident while running their game without appearing rude or too controlling. If needed, give the children alternative ways to get their point across to the group.

## Variations

Add additional guidelines to the game creation, such as putting a time limit on how long the game can take to play, etc.

# 4

# LANGUAGE AND LITERACY ACTIVITIES

# Instruction construction

## Aim

- To write instructions for others

- To read and follow written instructions

## Assessment opportunities

This activity will help identify children who struggle to communicate their thoughts and ideas in a written form.

## What you need

- A pile of building bricks – each pair should have matching pieces

- Paper or small whiteboards

- Pens or whiteboard markers

- Barrier boards

## ACTIVITY

Talk to the children about instruction writing – how it is important for the instructions to be short and clear. Discuss the use of 'bossy' words to help others understand what they need to do. For example, 'Take the yellow brick,' and 'Put the green brick on top of the blue brick.' Discuss the use of lists and bullet points, modelling how to do them on the paper or whiteboard.

Put the children into pairs. Each child should have four bricks and their bricks should be the same shape, size and colour as their partner's bricks.

Number the children 'Player 1' and 'Player 2' in their pairs. Both players should construct a small model with their bricks, behind the barrier boards, without their partner watching. They should then write the instructions for how to build their model on paper or a whiteboard. Remind them to use short, clear instructions and bullet points.

Ask Player 1 to pass their instructions to Player 2 and vice versa. They should take it in turns to attempt to build each other's models.

Remind the children it doesn't matter if they don't get it completely right – the important thing is to think about how to rewrite the instructions to be clearer for their partner.

Encourage the children to discuss in a group which kind of instructions worked best for them.

## Variations

The children could do the 'Listen and build' activity from Section 2 first to get them used to giving and receiving verbal instructions before writing them.

# Brick by brick poetry: listening

## Aim

- To listen to and discuss poetry

## Assessment opportunities

This activity will help identify children who struggle to speak articulately in full sentences.

## What you need

- Pile of bricks of different colours

- A colour poem (see Appendix for example)

## ACTIVITY

Each child has a pile of bricks with a mixture of colours.

Explain to the children that you are going to read something and they should listen carefully. When they hear a particular colour named, they should pick that colour up and start to put their pieces together in order.

Read the poem, modelling how to read using expression. Give the children time to process the words and find the correct coloured bricks.

When the poem is finished, ask the children to say what colours they heard and anything they remember about each colour in the poem. Ask the children to give examples of other things that the author could have had for each colour.

Read the poem again and get the children to point to the corresponding brick in their colour model, giving them a chance to finish each line, prompting if needed.

## Variations

Use colour word cards to practise reading the key words as they discuss them.

# Brick by brick poetry: reading

## Aim

- To listen to and read poetry

## Assessment opportunities

This activity will help identify children who struggle to read key words.

## What you need

- Pile of bricks of different colours

- Colour poem (see Appendix for example) on a large sheet of paper or whiteboard and also one copy for each child

- Colour brick model (built during 'Brick by brick poetry: listening' activity)

## ACTIVITY

Each child has their model or one you have made previously, using all the colours described in the poem.

Explain to the children that they are going to read the poem together, using their model to help.

Show the children the first line of the poem. Ask them to look at the words and see if they can find the colour word in the line and any other familiar words.

On their own copies, in pairs, ask them to underline all the words that they know in that line. Ask the pairs to read out the words they have found.

Read out the first line to the group and get the children to follow it on their copies. When the words they have underlined come up, they should read them out with you.

Continue with the next line and repeat the process of finding and reading out key words and then the whole line. They can remind themselves of the order of colours by looking at their building bricks model.

As the children become more confident, they can attempt to read out the lines themselves, after identifying the key words.

## Variations

Use word banks that are familiar to the children so they can match key words from the poem on their own word banks.

# Brick by brick poetry: composition and writing

### Aim

- To create poetry

### Assessment opportunities

This activity will help identify children who struggle to create poetry independently.

### What you need

- Pile of bricks of different colours
- Colour poem (see Appendix for example) on a large sheet of paper or whiteboard
- Colour brick model (built during 'Brick by brick poetry: listening' activity)

### ACTIVITY

Each child has their model or one you have made, using all the colour pieces described in the poem.

Read through the colour poem. If the children have completed the 'Brick by brick poetry: listening' and 'Brick by brick poetry: reading' activities, they may be familiar with the poem and should be encouraged to read along, pointing to their models as the colours are read.

Put a pile of a particular colour brick in the middle. Ask the children to think about what else is that colour brick. 'Collect' their ideas by writing them on a whiteboard or paper.

Repeat the same process with another colour.

Ask the children to work in pairs and have a pile of a particular colour in front of each pair, ie one pair has red, one pair has green, etc. Ask them to work together to think about things that are that colour.

The children should share their ideas with the facilitator 'collecting' them on the whiteboard or paper.

When there are ideas for at least six colours, read them out and the group should agree on a line for each colour.

Add exciting and interesting adjectives to the lines.

If appropriate for the group, pass the paper or whiteboard round and ask the children to add on their own line in their pairs. If a child can only add a few words, this is OK as long as they can have a go.

When the poem is complete, read it out as a group, adding actions or using their brick models to encourage adding expression.

## Variations

Use word banks that are familiar to the children so they can independently write the key words in their own poems.

# Story building: characters

## Aim

• Narrative composition – characters

## Assessment opportunities

This activity will help identify children who struggle to use descriptive words.

## What you need

• A bag of small figures

• A large piece of paper

• Sheets of A4 paper

• Blu-Tack

• Pencils and pens

## ACTIVITY

Ask the children to think about characters in stories and books. They can also think about real people.

Ask the children what words they might use to describe these characters and people. It may be a description of their appearance or personality. 'Collect' the words by writing them on the big piece of paper, drawing images next to each word to help those who struggle to read independently.

Pass the bag of figures round and ask the children to take one. They should look at their figure and think of a word to describe them. They can use a word that has already been 'collected' if they want, or come up with a new word.

Each child should take it in turns to hold up their character and say the word they have picked to describe it.

Each child should put some Blu-Tack on their character and attach it to the middle of their sheet of paper. They should write their word on the paper near their character.

Ask the children to write more words to describe their characters, using word banks if needed.

When the children have words to describe their character, ask them to give them a name and present their character to the group, encouraging the use of whole sentences while speaking.

Repeat the activity with another character, giving the children the opportunity for more independent work and less prompting.

Keep the characters on their paper and use them with other 'Story building' activities, or display them in the classroom.

Take photos of each character to use in 'Story building: writing' if appropriate.

## Variations
Children can do this activity in pairs if appropriate.

# Story building: settings

## Aim

- Narrative composition – settings

## Assessment opportunities

This activity will help identify children who struggle to recall settings from stories that have been read to them. It will also help identify those who find it difficult to use descriptive terms.

## What you need

- A pile of building bricks, vehicles and other pieces

- Pictures of settings from stories or real-life places

- A ready-built setting as an example

## ACTIVITY

Ask the children to think about settings. Discuss different books and stories they have read or heard and talk about where they are set.

Use the pictures to help prompt discussion and encourage the use of descriptive words. Talk about the atmosphere and what the surroundings would include, for example would there be wildlife or extra-terrestrial creatures?

Get the children to think about their ideal setting – would it be hot or cold, inside or outside, busy or quiet, etc. Tell them to build their setting with the building bricks and pieces. They can be as creative as they like.

Allow plenty of time for the children to build the model, prompting thinking by asking questions if they get stuck for ideas.

When the children have finished their models, ask them to describe their setting, pointing at important parts of their model. Encourage all children to ask questions about each other's models.

Take photos of the settings to use in 'Story building: writing' if appropriate.

## Variations

Children can build settings in pairs if appropriate.

# Story building: events

## Aim
• Narrative composition – sequencing events

## Assessment opportunities

This activity will help identify children who struggle to describe a sequence of events independently.

## What you need
• A pile of bricks, vehicles, figures and other pieces of building blocks for each child

• Pile of extra bricks and pieces in the middle of the group

• Time-related word bank (see Appendix)

• The characters used in the 'Story building: characters' activity if appropriate

• The settings created in the 'Story building: settings' activity if appropriate

• Other pre-made 'settings' if appropriate

## ACTIVITY
Each child should have their own character and setting or a figure and pre-prepared setting if this is a stand-alone activity. Discuss how things happen to characters in stories, giving examples of known stories.

With a figure and a building brick setting, model an event happening to some characters. Discuss how to make it exciting and how the characters may react to the event, depending on their personalities.

Get the children to do the same with their own characters and setting. If appropriate, the children can pair up and have an event happen to the characters at each setting.

When the children have had a chance to practise their events, ask them to present it to the group, 'walking' their character through the setting. You can encourage use of exciting and imaginative language, using word banks as appropriate.

If needed for further activities, take photos of each stage of the event for use later.

## Variations

A short story can be read at the beginning of this activity and the events in it highlighted and discussed to help the children be clear about how events are sequenced.

Speechmark Ⓢ

# Story building: writing

## Aim

- Narrative composition – writing a story

## Assessment opportunities

This activity will help identify children who struggle with recording their ideas in a written form.

## What you need

- Settings models from 'Story building: settings'

- Characters from 'Story building: characters'

- Photos of characters from 'Story building: characters'

- Photos of events from 'Story building: events'

- Word banks for descriptive language and time connectives

- Large pieces of paper

- Paper glue

- Pens and pencils

## ACTIVITY

Recap the previous activities, reminding the children about the characters and settings they have constructed. Remind the children of the descriptive words they used to make their characters and settings interesting.

Give the children the photos of their characters. Model putting the photo of a character on the large piece of paper and writing a few sentences, using the words they collected on their own pages during the activity. For example, 'Max was tall and very strong. His hair was as spiky as a hedgehog's back and his scowl made others move aside as he approached.' Ask the children to do the same with the photos of their characters. Ask the children to show the group and read what they have written.

Model doing a similar thing with the photos of the settings. For example, 'Max lived in the middle of a dark, lonely forest. The place smelt of rotting vegetables and many animals avoided going near it. The trees seemed to be whispering secrets to each other. At night, there were often strange noises.'

Get the children to do the same with their photos, sticking them next to their characters on their large piece of paper. Ask the children to read out what they've written to the group.

Give the children the photos of their sequence of events. Recap one of the stories, modelling putting the events into the right order on to the paper next to their character and settings. Get the children to do the same with their photos. Ask them to recall their story, pointing at each picture and describing it in whole sentences.

When the children are confident their photos are in the correct order, ask them to stick them on the paper.

Ask the children to write a sentence under each photo to describe what is happening. If they want to they can add speech and thought bubbles to add dialogue for the characters. Encourage the use of whole sentences and correct punctuation.

Ask the children to present their story to the group or their class, reading from each photo.

## Variations

Increase or decrease the amount of photos depending on the abilities of the children in the group.

Get the children to work in pairs to help each other create their stories.

# Build a sentence

## Aim

- To be able to communicate in whole sentences

## Assessment opportunities

This activity will help identify children who rely on communication through use of key words only.

## What you need

- Large, long rectangular bricks to form a base for their sentences

- Pile of bricks of different colours and shapes

## ACTIVITY

Talk about communicating with single words and how we can add more words to talk and write using whole sentences.

Put a long rectangular brick in the middle and say a sentence, eg 'I like eating bananas'. Pick up a brick to represent each word (preferably linking the size of the brick to the length of the word, so a small brick for 'I', etc).

Put the bricks in the correct order on the long rectangular one and ask the children to say the sentence again, pointing to the corresponding brick as each word is said.

Ask a child a question, eg 'What is your favourite colour?' If the child answers with a single word (eg 'Blue'), accept that is one word in their sentence and ask them to pick a brick that represents their word. Put it on the base in the correct place (not at the beginning of the sentence). Ask all the children to think about what other words can be added to turn the answer into a whole sentence. If they are unsure, model adding the other words 'I like the colour...' and adding appropriate bricks to form the whole sentence.

Repeat the activity a few times until the children start to use whole sentences and then let them have a go at building their own sentences individually or in pairs.

Ask the children to present their sentences to the group, using their model sentences to help them.

## Variations

To move on to writing, get the children to start to write their sentences with the building blocks model as a prompt.

# 5

# LANGUAGE AND NUMERACY ACTIVITIES

# Investigating counting 1

### Aim

- To be able to count up to 20

### Assessment opportunities

This activity will help identify children who are not confident in counting groups of objects.

### What you need

- Pile of bricks of the same size

- Number cards 1–20

### ACTIVITY

Each child has a pile of bricks.

Hold up the number cards in order and model counting the correct number of bricks. For example, hold up number '1' and place one brick on the card, then hold up number '2' and place two bricks on the card, etc. Ask the children to check if there is the correct number of bricks on each card.

Repeat again in order with the children finding the correct number of bricks for each card. Ask the children to check.

Next, hold up the number cards in a random order with the children finding the correct amount of bricks for each card. Ask them to discuss and think about what the size of the pile looks like and how the size of the pile changes with the different number of bricks.

Ask the children to repeat the activity in twos or independently, monitoring whether they are counting correctly.

### Variations

Be aware that some children may try to count the number of dots on top of the bricks. If this happens, only single dot bricks or pieces with no dots on should be used to avoid confusion.

# Investigating counting 2

## Aim

- To be able to count in steps of 2, 3, 4, 5 and 10

## Assessment opportunities

This activity will help identify children who are not confident in counting in steps.

## What you need

- A pile of bricks with different numbers of 'studs' or 'dots' on, including those with a single 'dot'

- Paper or small whiteboards

- Pens or whiteboard markers

## ACTIVITY

Put the pile of bricks and pieces in the middle.

Ask the children to find all the bricks with a single 'dot'. When they have found them, count them together. Write the sequence of numbers on a piece of paper or whiteboard.

Explain to the children that sometimes we can count quicker by counting in bigger steps. Ask them to find the pieces with two 'dots'. Model to the children how they can count in twos with these pieces and write up the sequence of numbers, eg 2, 4, 6, 8, etc.

Ask the children to make groups of threes by adding a single 'dot' to a brick with two 'dots'. Ask them to use these pieces to count in 3s. Write out the sequence of numbers.

Let the children try different ways to count, adding different pieces together or finding pieces with the same amount of 'dots'. Ask them to write the sequences on their paper. Make sure the children are clear that they should always use bricks with the same amount of 'dots'.

Ask them to show their findings to the group, laying out their bricks and counting in their chosen number.

## Variations

If this is too difficult, the activity can focus on counting in 2s first and move on to other numbers once the children are confident.

# Sum language 1

## Aim

- To be able to use basic language of addition and subtraction

## Assessment opportunities

This activity will help identify children who do not understand the language being used with addition and subtraction tasks.

## What you need

- Pile of bricks of the same size

- 'Sum language 1' cards (see Appendix)

## ACTIVITY

Show the children the 'addition' sign. Ask them to tell you all the words they know that link to this sign. Correct any misunderstandings. Discuss what it means and the different ways they may hear it used in the classroom and at home. Show them the vocabulary card. Add more terms as appropriate.

Make an equation from the bricks, using the 'addition' and 'equals' signs. For example, 1 brick + 2 bricks = 3 bricks. Model doing the same thing with different numbers of bricks, using the vocabulary and encouraging the children to say it out loud at the same time.

Ask the children to work in pairs to create their own sums using the signs. Ask the children to show the group, encouraging them to use the correct vocabulary to describe their sum.

Show the children the 'subtraction' sign. Again, ask them to tell you all the words that link to this sign. Discuss its meaning and uses, giving examples they can relate to. Show them the vocabulary card.

Make an equation using bricks and the 'subtraction' and 'equals' signs. Using the vocabulary and modelling the method, discuss how there will be 'fewer' bricks if you are taking them away.

Ask the children to create their own subtraction sums in pairs. They should present to the group, using the appropriate vocabulary.

## Variations

When appropriate, the children can start to write out their equations on paper or whiteboards.

# Sum language 2

### Aim

- To be able to use basic language of multiplication and division

### Assessment opportunities

This activity will help identify children who do not understand the language being used with multiplication and division tasks.

### What you need

- Pile of bricks of the same size

- 'Sum language 2' cards (see Appendix)

### ACTIVITY

Show the children the 'multiply' sign. Ask them to tell you all the words they know that link to this sign. Correct any misunderstandings. Discuss what it means and the different ways they may hear it used in the classroom and at home. Show them the vocabulary card.

Give the children four bricks. Ask the children to group the bricks into twos. Use the vocabulary to explain they now have two lots of twos.

Give the children six bricks. Ask them to group them into twos. Ask them how many lots of twos they have got now.

Repeat with different numbers of bricks and larger numbers in each group. Use the number cards and the multiplication and equals cards to model how these equations can be presented.

Set out the groups of bricks in an array, so the children can start to see patterns as they add more groups to the array.

Ask the children to work in pairs to create their own groups. Let them investigate using different numbers of bricks and encourage them to look for patterns. Ask them to present what they have found to the group, using the appropriate vocabulary.

Show the children the 'division' sign. Again, ask them to tell you all the words that link to this sign. Discuss its meaning and uses, giving examples they can relate to. Show them the vocabulary card.

Ask the children to get into pairs. Give each pair a pile of bricks and ask them to divide them equally between them. Talk about how the bricks have been divided equally between two. How many did each person get? Model how to use the correct language to present this, eg 20 bricks divided by 2 equals 10. Ask the children to get into threes and repeat the dividing up of the bricks. If appropriate, there may be a number of bricks bricks left over. Help the children understand that the bricks left over are 'remainders'. Use the number cards and the division and equals cards to model how these equations can be presented.

Give the children a pile of bricks and get them to have a go at dividing up different amounts of bricks, looking for patterns and using the correct vocabulary.

## Variations
When appropriate, the children can start to write out their equations on paper or whiteboards.

# Position the piece

## Aim

- To use the language of position

## Assessment opportunities

This activity will help identify children who are not using positional language correctly.

## What you need

- A variety of bricks with enough of the same ones for each child
- Positional word bank (See Appendix for example)

## ACTIVITY

Give each child the same kinds of bricks – each child will only need about six bricks of different colours. You should have a pile too.

Talk through the positional language you want the children to use: 'on top of', 'underneath', 'next to', 'near', 'far', etc.

Give the children some instructions, modelling the meaning with your own bricks:

- 'Put the blue brick on top of the green brick'
- 'Put the yellow brick underneath the red brick'
- 'Put the yellow brick between the red brick and the blue brick'
- 'Put the orange brick next to the white brick'
- 'Put the red brick far from all the other bricks'

Continue to give instructions and get the children to copy.

Start to give instructions without modelling, so the children are responding to the verbal information.

When confident, get the children to give instructions together.

## Variations

If needed, introduce only one key word at a time.

# Explain the position 1

### Aim

- To use the language of position

### Assessment opportunities

This activity will help identify children who are not using positional language correctly.

### What you need

- Camera
- Laminator
- Pile of bricks
- Positional word bank (see Appendix for example)

## ACTIVITY

### *Making the cards*

First the group will make themselves some activity cards. Get the children to place a few bricks in different groups in front of them. Some can be on top of each other and others next to each other on the table. Help the children take photos of their groups. They could work in pairs to help each other.

Print out the photos, laminate them and make them into activity cards to play with.

### *Playing the game*

Put the pile of bricks and pieces in the middle. Make sure the same pieces are available as are on your cards.

Talk through the positional language you want the children to use, modelling the meaning of the words using building blocks. For example, 'The red block is on top of the blue block.' A word bank can also be used.

Pick up an activity card, and describe the pieces and how they are positioned. Tell the children to listen carefully and place their pieces as you describe. If some children are likely to rely on watching others to complete the task, make sure the children take it in turns and complete the task independently as they become more confident with the language.

When they are confident, get the children to use the cards with each other, describing the pieces and how they are positioned. Monitor and correct language use as appropriate.

## Variations
If needed, introduce only one key word at a time.

# Explain the position 2

## Aim

- To use the language of position

## Assessment opportunities

This activity will help identify children who are not using positional language correctly.

## What you need

- Camera

- Laminator

- A pile of bricks for each child

- Positional word bank (see Appendix for example) – above, between, around, near, close and far

## ACTIVITY

### Making the cards (prepare beforehand if necessary)

First the group will make themselves some activity cards. Get the children to place a few bricks in different groups in front of them. Talk about how the bricks are above, between, near, close to and far away from other bricks. Help the children to take photos of their groups. They could work in pairs to help each other.

Print out the photos, laminate them and make them into activity cards to play with.

### Playing the game

Put the pile of bricks and pieces in the middle.

Talk through the language you want the children to use, modelling the meaning of the words using building blocks. For example, 'The green block is near the yellow block with four red blocks around them.'

Pick up one of your activity cards, and describe the pieces and how they are positioned. Tell the children to listen carefully and place their pieces as you describe. As with the 'Explain the position 1' activity, make sure the children take it in turns to make sure all children are understanding the words.

When they are confident, get the children to use the cards with each other, describing the pieces and how they are positioned. Monitor and correct language use as appropriate.

## Variations

If needed, introduce only one key word at a time.

# Direct me

### Aim

- To use the language of direction and motion

### Assessment opportunities

This activity will help identify children who are not using directional language correctly.

### What you need

- A pile of bricks for each child

- Directional word bank (see Appendix for example)

- Colour cards

- Blindfolds

### ACTIVITY

Talk through the directional words, modelling the meaning of the words using building blocks, eg 'I'm moving this piece up.' Give the children a building brick each and get them to have a go together, checking to see that they understand the terms. Get them to move their brick 'up', 'down', 'left', 'right', etc.

Spread the colour cards out on the table. Ask for a volunteer who will help model the activity. Put the blindfold on them and give them a building block. Using the directional words, guide the child to the colour card that corresponds with the colour of the block the child has. Get them to take off their blindfold to check they have correctly followed the instructions. The objective is to place the brick on the matching colour card, for example, all the blue bricks near the blue card, and so on.

The children will need to understand that 'left' and 'right' will be different for the other person if they are facing them. If the children do not have this understanding, make sure the person directing is facing the same way as their partner when giving directions.

Put the children in pairs and give them a selection of bricks. Explain that they are going to direct their partner to put the bricks on the correct cards.

Monitor their use of language and correct as appropriate.

## Variations

To create more opportunities for using 'up', the colour cards can be placed on items at different levels across the table.

This activity can also be done across a larger area, using coloured hula hoops or mats instead of colour cards

# Describe me in 3D

### Aim

- To identify and describe properties of 3D shapes, particularly cuboids and cubes (edges, vertices and faces)

### Assessment opportunities

This activity will help identify children who are not confident using vocabulary associated with 3D shapes.

### What you need

- Pile of bricks, including irregular shapes if available

- 3D shapes word bank (see Appendix for example)

### ACTIVITY

Pick up a brick and, using the vocab cards, explain the meaning of 'edges', 'vertices' and 'faces'.

Ask a child to have a go at describing a piece using these words. In pairs they should all have a go at describing a piece.

The children should create a small model each and challenge their partner to describe some of its properties to the rest of the group, eg 'this shape has eight faces and 10 vertices' or 'this shape has one curved face and one flat face'.

Challenge the children to create models which have particular properties.

### Variations

Add further language such as 'parallel', 'right angle', 'symmetry'.

# Organise and classify 1

### Aim
- To be able to classify and organise information

### Assessment opportunities
This activity will help identify children who are not able to identify features and classify into groups.

### What you need
- Pile of bricks and pieces

- Venn diagram activity card (see Appendix for example)

### ACTIVITY
Explain to the children that they are going to classify the bricks and put them into groups according to their features.

Show them the Venn diagram card and explain that some pieces will fit into one circle and others will fit into the other circle. Other pieces may have features of both groups. They will need to be placed in the section where the two circles overlap. There will also be pieces that don't fit into either of the circles and these can be placed outside the diagram.

Give the children a pile of bricks and pieces and ask them to put them in the correct area on the diagram. Encourage them to discuss the features of the pieces and allow them to sort all the pieces before checking together.

Give the children the opportunity to change any of their choices as they start to check.

### Variations
Repeat the same activity with other features in the diagram or add another circle to the diagram to include another category.

# Organise and classify 2

### Aim

- To be able to classify and organise information and explain their reasoning

### Assessment opportunities

This activity will help identify children who are not able to identify features and classify into groups.

### What you need

- Pile of bricks and pieces

- Carroll diagram (see Appendix for example)

### ACTIVITY

Explain to the children that they are going to classify the bricks and put them into groups according to their features.

Show them the Carroll diagram and explain that they will need to place the pieces in the correct box based on the features of the bricks. For example, if a brick is blue and has four dots it will go in one box but if it is blue with six dots it will go in the box below.

Let the children sort the pieces, encouraging discussion about the features and reasons for their choices. When all the pieces have been sorted, check the decisions the children have made.

Give the children the opportunity to change any of their choices as they start to check.

### Variations

Repeat the same activity with other features in the diagram.

# APPENDIX: TEMPLATES AND RESOURCES

# A colour poem

Red

Red is the soft rose petal that unfolds beneath the summer sunshine

Blue

Blue is the sky; the sky that appears boldly after the rain, forcing the clouds to move on

Green

Green is the grass on the ground, the leaves on the trees and the frogs splashing into my pond

White

White is the potato Mum lets me mash on a Monday when I get home

Pink

Pink are the tiny fingers on my baby sister's hand; miniature versions of my own that curl tightly

Orange

Orange is the juice that I catch in my cup as it flows from the bottle like a colourful stream

Brown

Brown is the mud. The squidgy, squashy, filthy, messy mud that oozes through my toes

Yellow

Yellow is the sour tasting lemon that makes my face fizz

*(Amy Eleftheriades)*

# Building blocks session checklist

1   Group welcome – saying hello and welcoming new people

2   Warm-up game

3   Buzz-in game

4   Describe the pieces

5   Free choice

6   Clear up

# Building bricks bingo grid

|  |  |  |
|---|---|---|
|  |  |  |
|  |  |  |
|  |  |  |
|  |  |  |

# Description cards

| | |
|---|---|
| **big** | **small** |
| **narrow** | **wide** |
| **short** | **tall** |
| | |

# Listen and build cards

## Listen and build

Create a model using:

2 green bricks

2 yellow bricks

1 red brick

## Listen and build

Create a model using:

6 blue bricks

4 red bricks

5 white bricks

2 green bricks

## Listen and build

Create a model using:

10 red bricks

8 yellow bricks

3 orange bricks

2 cubes (any colour)

3 irregular shapes
(any colour)

## Listen and build

Create a model using:

4 long, red bricks

3 small, green bricks

2 big, black bricks

3 more bricks (free choice)

## Listen and build

Create a model using:


2 blue bricks

3 black bricks


## Listen and build

Create a model using:


5 orange bricks

4 yellow bricks

2 bricks with 4 studs
(dots)


## Listen and build

Create a model using:


6 bricks with 8 studs
(dots)

3 bricks with more than 2
studs (dots)

4 blue bricks

2 bricks with no studs
(dots)


## Listen and build

Create a model using:


One of each colour that
matches the clothes you
are wearing today

# Numeracy: Carroll diagram (blank)

| | | |
|---|---|---|
| | | |
| | | |
| | | |

# Numeracy: Carroll diagram 1

| Green | | |
|---|---|---|
| **Red** | | |
| | **More than six faces** | **Less than six faces** |

# Numeracy: Carroll diagram 2

| | Blue | White |
|---|---|---|
| **Studs (dots)** | | |
| **No studs (dots)** | | |

  Speechmark

# Numeracy: Venn diagram 1

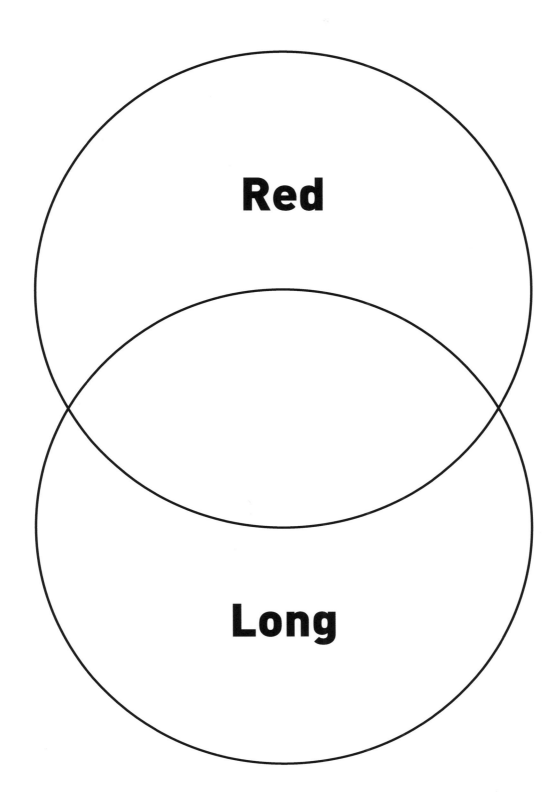

# Numeracy: Venn diagram 2

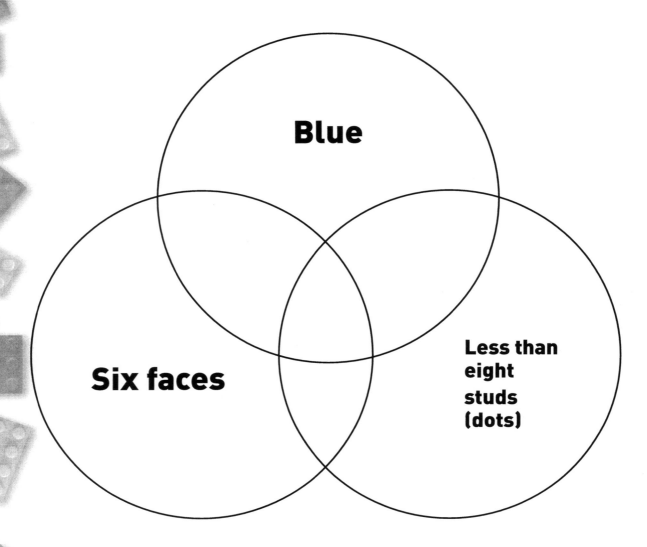

## Please can you pass me ...

Please can you pass me a

_____ piece

with _____ studs on top.

Please can you pass me

_____ pieces.

Please can you pass me

_____

# Please can you pass me a blue piece.

# Please can you pass me a red piece.

# Please can you pass me a green piece.

# Secret challenge cards

## My Secret Challenge Card

1 To try to say polite and helpful things during the games.

**Please**      **Thank you**      **Sorry**      **Can I help you?**

2 To take some time out when I feel I am getting cross with myself.

☺☺☺☺☺☺☺☺☺☺☺☺☺☺☺☺☺☺☺☺☺☺

## My Secret Challenge Card

1 To try to use these words in the games:

**long**            **short**            **big**            **small**

2 To try to wait until others have finished talking before I speak.

☺☺☺☺☺☺☺☺☺☺☺☺☺☺☺☺☺☺☺☺☺☺

## My Secret Challenge Card

1 To keep my head up when I'm talking and look towards the person I am talking to.

2 To have a go at saying my opinion, even if I am worried about what others think.

☺☺☺☺☺☺☺☺☺☺☺☺☺☺☺☺☺☺☺☺☺☺

# Sum language 1

**put together**

**add**

**altogether**

**plus**

**take away**

**distance between**

**difference between**

**subtract**

**minus**

**Sum language 1**

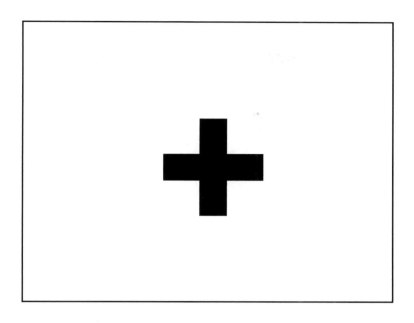

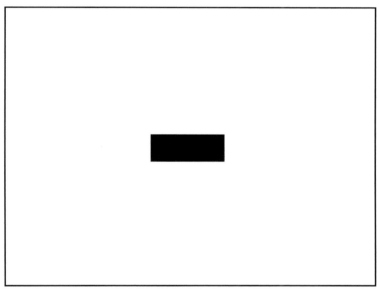

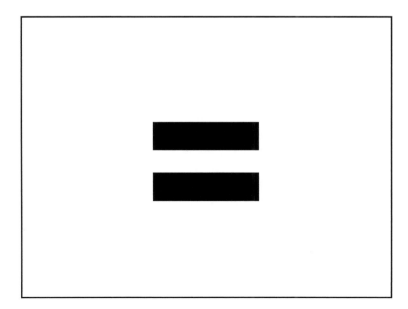

# Sum language 2

**lots of**

**groups of**

**times**

**multiply**

**multiplied by**

**share equally**

**divide**

**divided by**

**divided into**

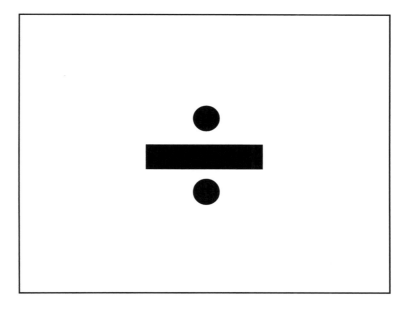

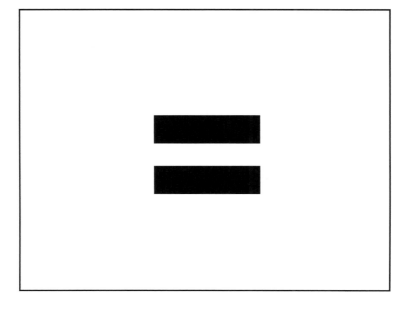

# Team speak

When we work in a team, there are different things we can say to give our opinions and help keep our team feeling good.

'It might be a good idea if ...'

'What do you think about ...'

'I'd like to do this, what do you think?'

'I'm impressed with that."

'I like the way you have ...'

'I don't like that idea as much as this one.'

'What a brilliant idea, nice one!'

'I understand what you're saying, but I prefer it this way.'

'Maybe we can find a way to include both our ideas.'

'This might be hard, but we'll get there!'

'Shall we take a break and come back to it later?'

# The negotiator script cards

| | |
|---|---|
| I would like ... | Please can I swap ...? |
| This piece here is really good, would you like to swap it for ...? | If I was to have that piece of yours, what would you like of mine? |
| How about these pieces for that one? | Yes, I agree with that swap! |
| Thank you for the offer but I don't want to swap that piece. | No thanks, but how about swapping for this piece? |
| What else might you want to swap for this piece? | Thanks but no thanks. |

# Word banks

## Position

| | | |
|---|---|---|
| next to | on top of | behind |
| under | inside | near |
| around | between | beside |
| outside | off | on |
| in front | up | down |
| left | right | |
| | | |
| | | |

## Colours

| | | |
|---|---|---|
| red | blue | yellow |
| white | black | pink |
| purple | orange | green |
| grey | brown | |
| | | |
| | | |
| | | |
| | | |

## Time

| | | |
|---|---|---|
| now | then | afterwards |
| finally | first | meanwhile |
| later on | after a while | soon |
| next | | |
| | | |
| | | |
| | | |
| | | |

Speechmark ⑤

## Numbers

| | | |
|---|---|---|
| one | two | three |
| four | five | six |
| seven | eight | nine |
| ten | eleven | twelve |
| thirteen | fourteen | fifteen |
| sixteen | seventeen | eighteen |
| nineteen | twenty | |
| | | |

## 3D shapes

| | | |
|---|---|---|
| cube | cuboid | sphere |
| triangular prism | square-based pyramid | cone |
| cylinder | edge | vertices |
| face | parallel | perpendicular |
| flat | curved | |
| | | |
| | | |
| | | |

## Maths

| | | |
|---|---|---|
| add | subtract | multiply |
| divide | decrease | difference |
| reduce | sum | product |
| times | share | take |
| minus | total | together |
| more | less | fewer |
| groups | remainder | double |
| | | |